AF205249

Impressum
Verlag: BABADADA GmbH, Nedderfeld 112 , 22529 Hamburg
Geschäftsführer / Verlags eitung: Harald Hof
Druck: Books on Demand GmbH, In de Tarpen 42, 22848 Norderstedt

Imprint
Publisher: BABADADA GmbH, Nedderfeld 112 , 22529 Hamburg, Germany
Managing Director / Publishing direction: Harald Hof
Print: Books on Demand GmbH, In de Tarpen 42, 22848 Norderstedt

Schule
school

Klassenzimmer
classroom

dividieren
divide

$186/2$

Tafel
board

Schulhof
school yard

Lehrer
teacher

Papier
paper

schreiben
write

Stift
pen

Schreibtisch
desk

Lineal
ruler

Buch
book

Schüler
pupil

Ranzen

satchel

Federmappe

pencil case

Bleistift

pencil

Bleistiftanspitzer

pencil sharpener

Radiergummi

rubber

Zeichenblock

drawing pad

Zeichnung
drawing

Pinsel
paintbrush

Malkasten
paint box

Schere
scissors

Klebstoff
glue

Übungsheft
exercise book

Hausaufgabe
homework

Zahl
number

addieren
add

subtrahieren
subtract

multiplizieren
multiply

rechnen
calculate

Buchstabe
letter

Alphabet
alphabet

Wort
word

Text

text

lesen

read

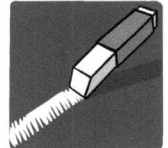

Kreide

chalk

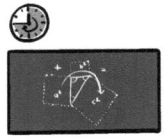

Stunde

lesson

Klassenbuch

register

Prüfung

examination

Zeugnis

certificate

Schuluniform

school uniform

Ausbildung

education

Lexikon

encyclopedia

Universität

university

Mikroskop

microscope

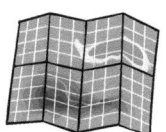

Karte

map

Papierkorb

waste-paper basket

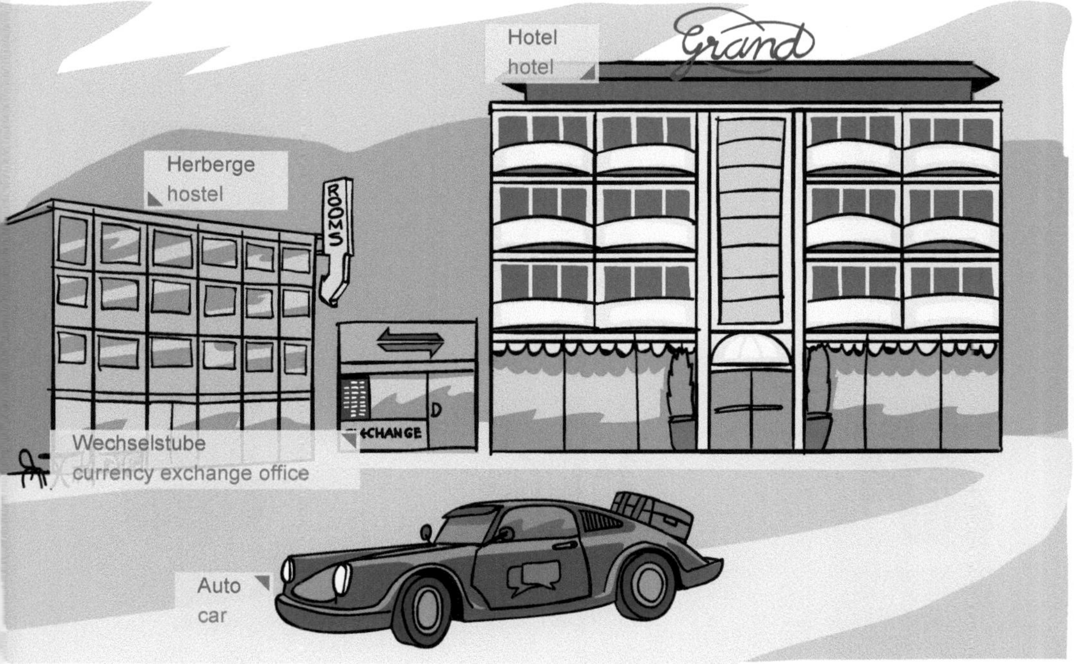

Hotel
hotel

Grand

Herberge
hostel

ROOMS

Wechselstube
currency exchange office

EXCHANGE

Auto
car

Sprache

language

ja / nein

yes / no

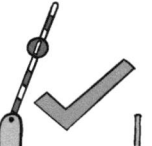

Okay

Okay

Hallo

hello

Übersetzer

translator

Danke

Thank you

Was kostet…?

how much is…?

Ich verstehe nicht

I don´t get it

Problem

problem

Guten Abend!

Good evening!

Guten Morgen!

Good morning!

Gute Nacht!

Good night!

Auf Wiedersehen

goodbye

Richtung

direction

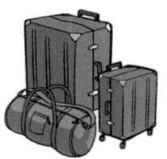

Gepäck

luggage

Tasche

bag

Rucksack

backpack

Gast

guest

Zimmer

room

Schlafsack

sleeping bag

Zelt

tent

Touristeninformation

tourist information

Strand

beach

Kreditkarte

credit card

Frühstück

breakfast

Mittagessen

lunch

Abendessen

dinner

Fahrkarte

Ticket

Fahrstuhl

elevator

Briefmarke

stamp

Grenze

border

Zoll

customs

Botschaft

embassy

Visum

visa

Pass

passport

Transport
transport

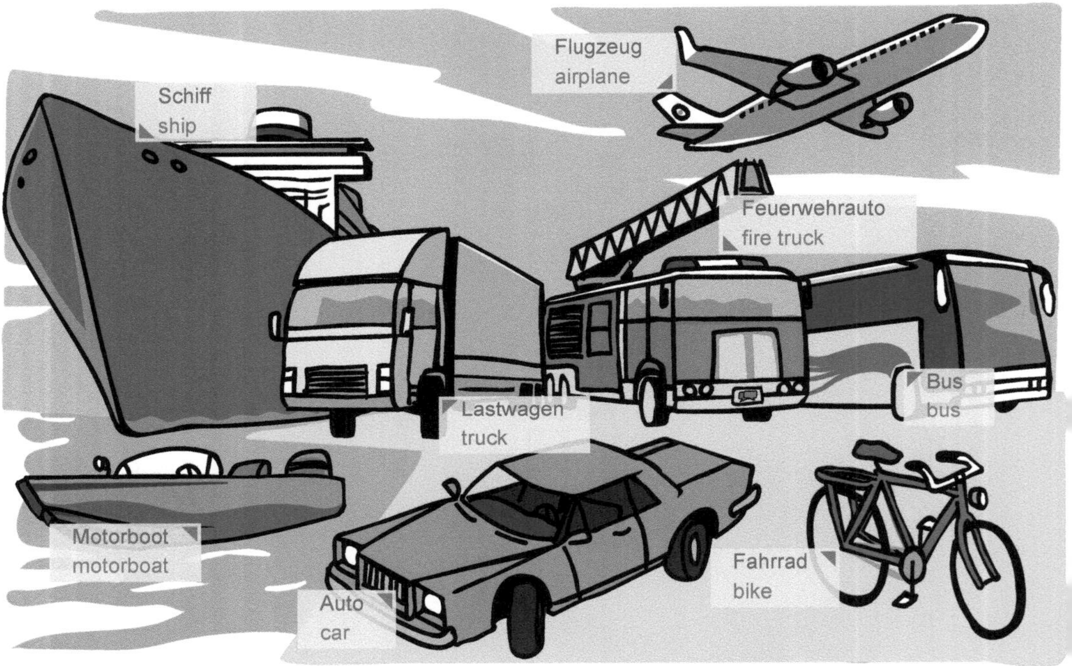
Flugzeug
airplane
Schiff
ship
Feuerwehrauto
fire truck
Bus
bus
Lastwagen
truck
Motorboot
motorboat
Fahrrad
bike
Auto
car

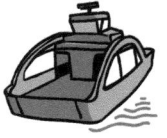

Fähre

ferry

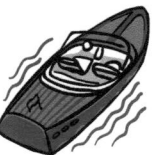

Boot

boat

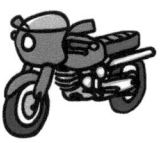

Motorrad

motorbike

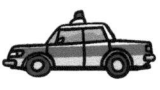

Polizeiauto

police car

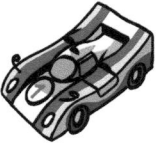

Rennauto

racing car

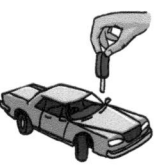

Mietwagen

rental car

Carsharing

car sharing

Abschleppwagen

tow truck

Müllauto

garbage truck

Motor

engine

Kraftstoff

fuel

Tankstelle

fuel station

Verkehrsschild

traffic sign

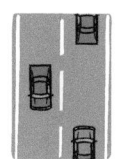

Verkehr

traffic

Stau

traffic jam

Parkplatz

parking lot

Bahnhof

train station

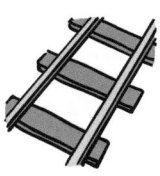

Schienen

tracks

Zug

train

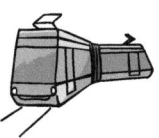

Straßenbahn

tram

Wagon

wagon

Helikopter

helicopter

Flughafen

airport

Tower

tower

Passagier

passenger

Container

container

Karton

carton

Karren

cart

Korb

basket

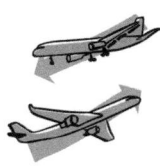

starten / landen

take off / land

Stadt

city

Dorf

village

Stadtzentrum

city center

Haus

house

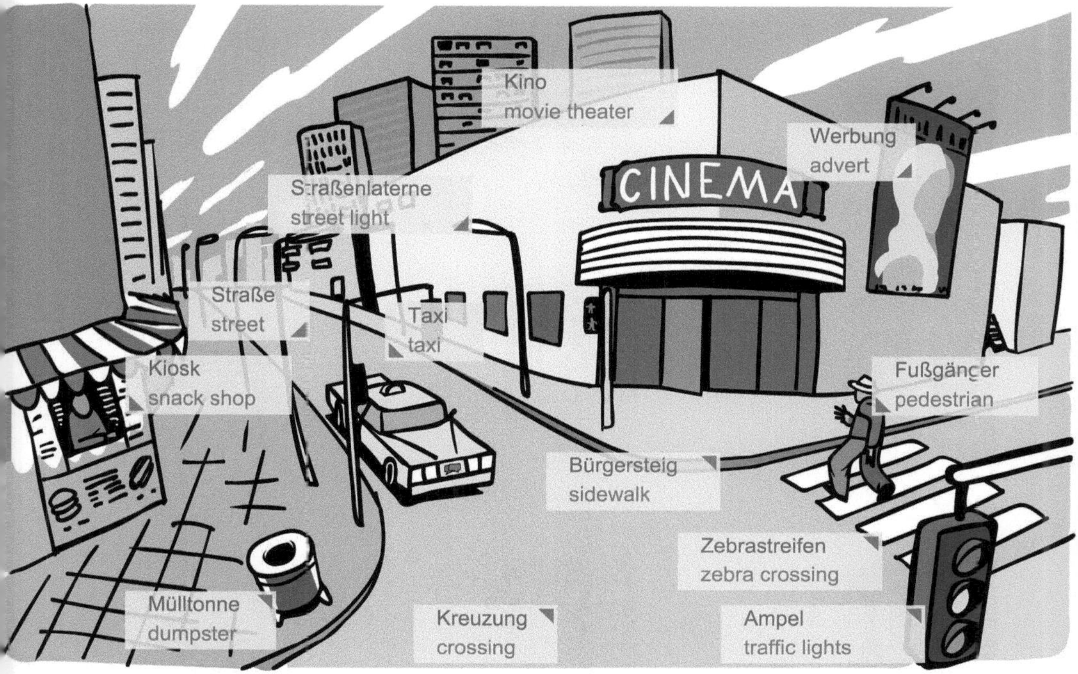

Kino
movie theater

Werbung
advert

Straßenlaterne
street light

CINEMA

Straße
street

Taxi
taxi

Kiosk
snack shop

Fußgänger
pedestrian

Bürgersteig
sidewalk

Zebrastreifen
zebra crossing

Mülltonne
dumpster

Kreuzung
crossing

Ampel
traffic lights

Hütte
hut

Wohnung
apartment

Bahnhof
train station

Rathaus
city hall

Museum
museum

Schule
school

Universität

university

Bank

bank

Krankenhaus

hospital

Hotel

hotel

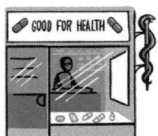

Apotheke

pharmacy

Büro

office

Buchhandlung

book shop

Geschäft

shop

Blumenladen

flower shop

Supermarkt

supermarket

Markt

market

Kaufhaus

department store

Fischhändler

fishmonger's shop

Einkaufszentrum

mall

Hafen

harbor

Park

park

Bank

bench

Brücke

bridge

Treppe

stairs

U-Bahn

subway

Tunnel

tunnel

Bushaltestelle

bus stop

Bar

bar

Restaurant

restaurant

Briefkasten

postbox

Straßenschild

street sign

Parkuhr

parking meter

Zoo

zoo

Badeanstalt

swimming pool

Moschee

mosque

Bauernhof

farm

Umweltverschmutzung

pollution

Friedhof

cemetery

Kirche

church

Spielplatz

playground

Tempel

temple

Landschaft
landscape

Wegweiser
signpost

Weg
path

Wiese
meadow

Stein
stone

Baum
tree

Wanderer
hiker

Fluss
river

Gras
grass

Blume
flower

Tal

valley

Berg

hill

See

lake

Wald

forest

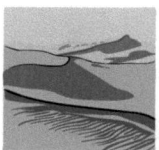

Wüste

desert

Vulkan

volcano

Schloss

castle

Regenbogen

rainbow

Pilz

mushroom

Palme

palm tree

Moskito

mosquito

Fliege

fly

Ameise

ant

Biene

bee

Spinne

spider

Käfer

beetle

Frosch

frog

Eichhörnchen

squirrel

Igel

hedgehog

Hase

hare

Eule

owl

Vogel

bird

Schwan

swan

Wildschwein

boar

Hirsch

deer

Elch

moose

Staudamm

dam

Windrad

wind turbine

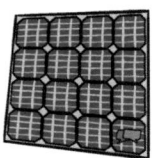

Solarmodul

solar panel

Klima

climate

Restaurant
restaurant

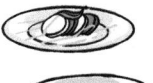

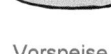

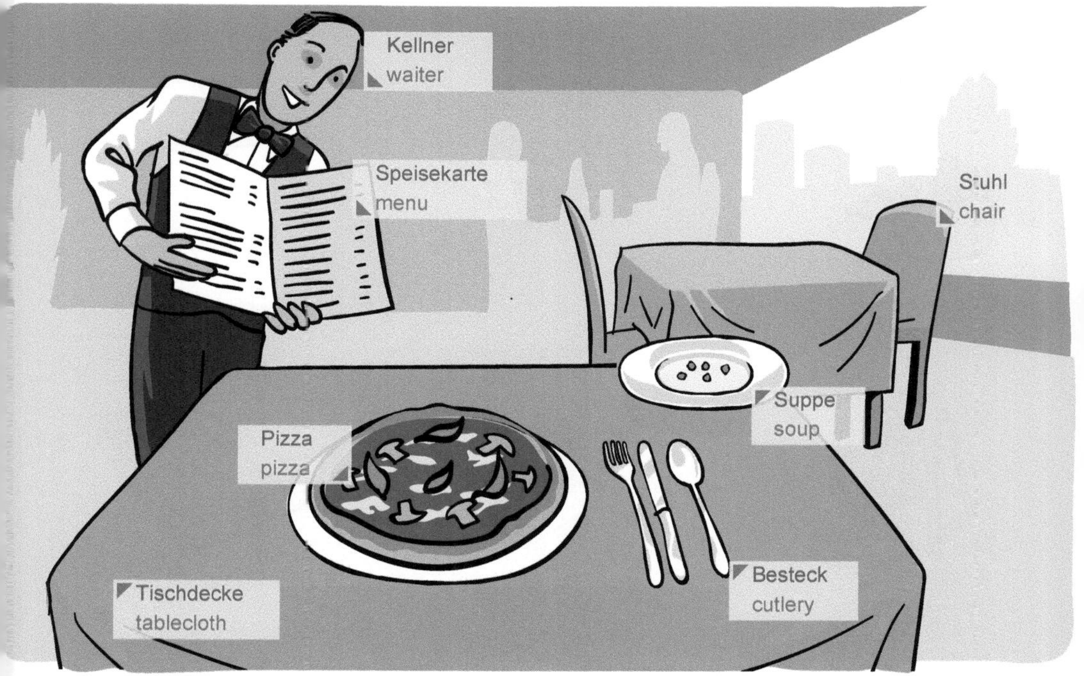
Kellner
waiter
Speisekarte
menu
Stuhl
chair
Suppe
soup
Pizza
pizza
Besteck
cutlery
Tischdecke
tablecloth

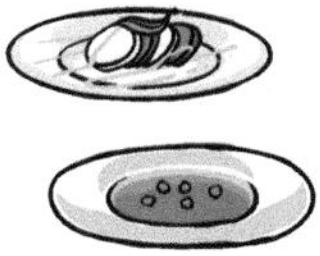

Vorspeise

starter

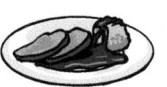

Hauptgericht

main course

Nachspeise

dessert

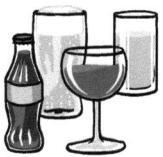

Getränke

drinks

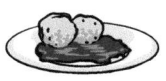

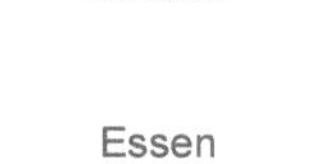

Essen

food

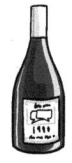

Flasche

bottle

Fastfood

fast food

Streetfood

street food

Teekanne

teapot

Zuckerdose

sugar bowl

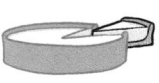

Portion

portion

Espressomaschine

espresso machine

Hochstuhl

high chair

Rechnung

bill

Tablett

tray

Messer

knife

Gabel

fork

Löffel

spoon

Teelöffel

teaspoon

Serviette

serviette

Glas

glass

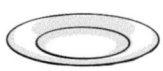		
Teller	Suppenteller	Untertasse
plate	soup plate	saucer

	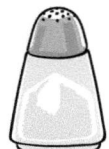	
Sauce	Salzstreuer	Pfeffermühle
sauce	salt shaker	pepper mill

		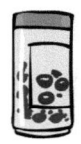 
Essig	Öl	Gewürze
vinegar	oil	spices

Ketchup	Senf	Mayonnaise
ketchup	mustard	mayonnaise

Supermarkt

supermarket

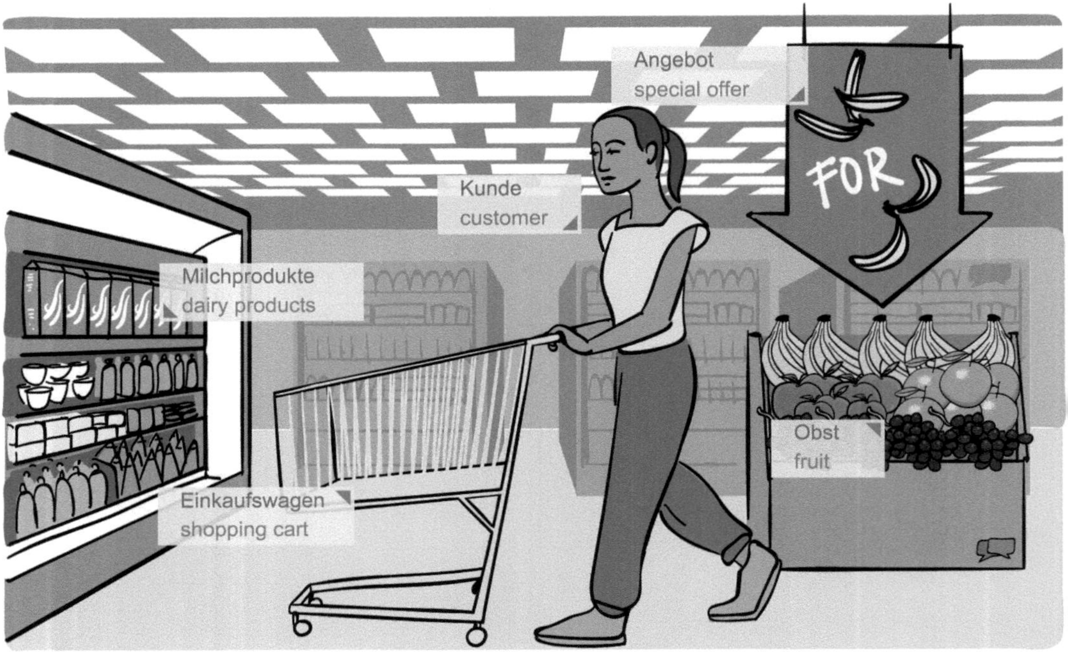

Angebot
special offer
FOR
Kunde
customer
Milchprodukte
dairy products
Obst
fruit
Einkaufswagen
shopping cart

BUTCHERS

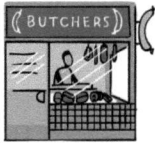

Schlachterei

butcher's shop

BAKERY

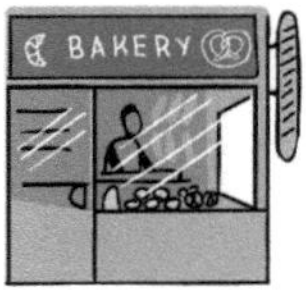

Bäckerei

bakery

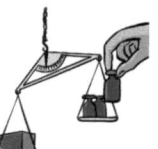

wiegen

weigh

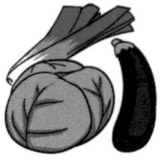

Gemüse

vegetables

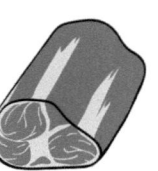

Fleisch

meat

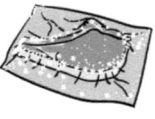

Tiefkühlkost

frozen food

Aufschnitt

cold cuts

Konserven

canned food

Waschmittel

detergent

Süßigkeiten

candy

Haushaltsartikel

household products

Reinigungsmittel

cleaning products

Verkäuferin

sales representative

Kasse

cash register

Kassierer

cashier

Einkaufsliste

shopping list

Öffnungszeiten

opening hours

Brieftasche

wallet

Kreditkarte

credit card

Tasche

bag

Plastiktüte

plastic bag

Wasser

water

Saft

juice

Milch

milk

Cola

coke

Wein

wine

Bier

beer

Alkohol

alcohol

Kakao

cocoa

Tee

tea

Kaffee

coffee

Espresso

espresso

Cappuccino

cappuccino

Banane

banana

Apfel

apple

Orange

orange

Melone

melon

Zitrone

lemon

Karotte

carrot

Knoblauch

garlic

Bambus

bamboo

Zwiebel

onion

Pilz

mushroom

Nüsse

nuts

Nudeln

noodles

Spaghetti

spaghetti

Reis

rice

Salat

salad

Pommes frites

fries

Bratkartoffeln

fried potatoes

Pizza

pizza

Hamburger

hamburger

Sandwich

sandwich

Schnitzel

escalope

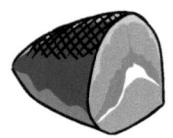

Schinken

ham

Salami

salami

Wurst

sausage

Huhn

chicken

Braten

roast

Fisch

fish

Haferflocken	Müsli	Cornflakes
porridge oats	muesli	cornflakes

Mehl	Croissant	Brötchen
flour	croissant	bread roll

Brot	Toast	Kekse
bread	toast	cookies

Butter	Quark	Kuchen
butter	curd	cake
		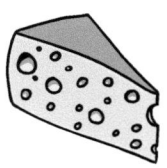
Ei	Spiegelei	Käse
egg	fried egg	cheese

Eiscreme

ice cream

Zucker

sugar

Honig

honey

Marmelade

jelly

Nougat-Creme

nougat cream

Curry

curry

Ziege

goat

Kuh

cow

Kalb

calf

Schwein

pig

Ferkel

piglet

Bulle

bull

Gans

goose

Ente

duck

Küken

chick

Huhn

hen

Hahn

cockerel

Ratte

rat

Katze

cat

Maus

mouse

Ochse

ox

Hund

dog

Hundehütte

dog house

Gartenschlauch

garden hose

Gießkanne

watering can

Sense

scythe

Pflug

plow

Sichel

sickle

Hacke

hoe

Mistgabel

pitchfork

Axt

axe

Schubkarre

pushcart

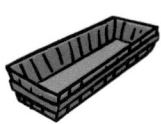

Trog

trough

Milchkanne

milk can

Sack

sack

Zaun

fence

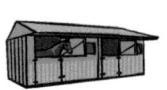

Stall

stable

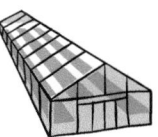

Treibhaus

greenhouse

Boden

soil

Saat

seed

Dünger

fertilizer

Mähdrescher

combine harvester

ernten

harvest

Ernte

harvest

Yamswurzel

yams

Weizen

wheat

Soja

soya

Kartoffel

potato

Mais

corn

Raps

rapeseed

Obstbaum

fruit tree

Maniok

manioc

Getreide

grain

Haus

house

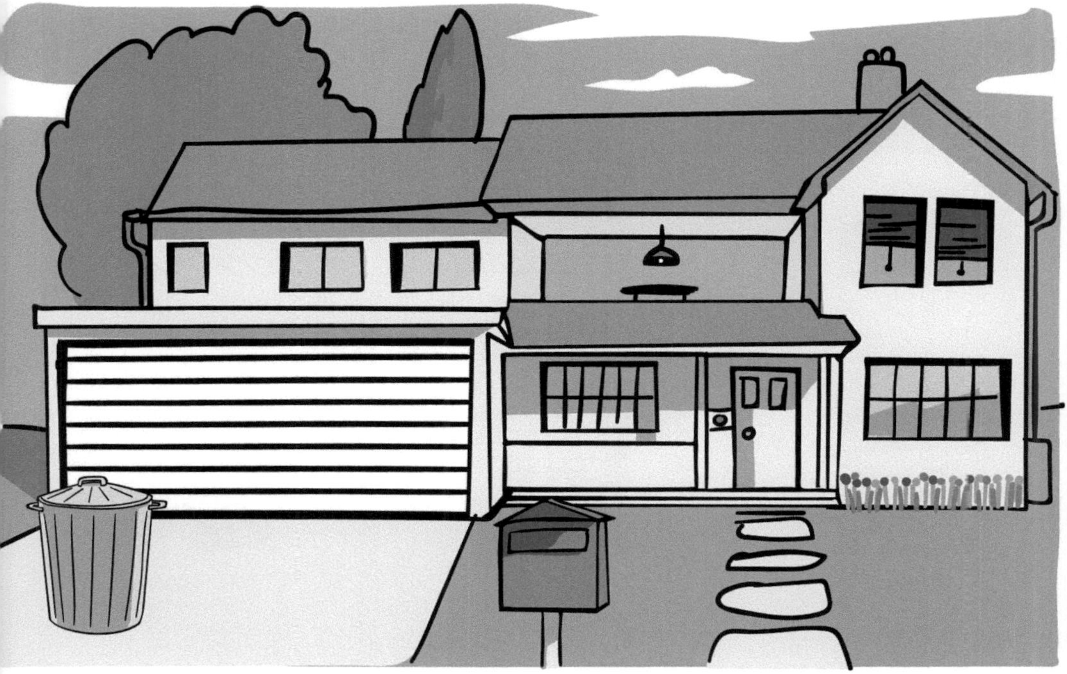

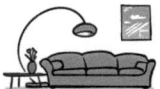

Wohnzimmer

living room

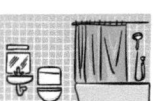

Badezimmer

bathroom

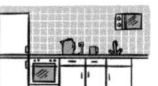

Küche

kitchen

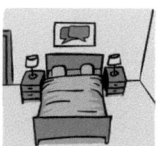

Schlafzimmer

bedroom

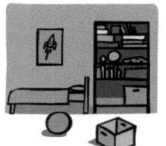

Kinderzimmer

kids room

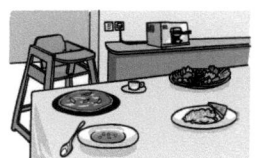

Esszimmer

dining room

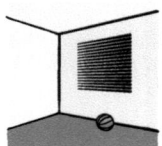

Boden

floor

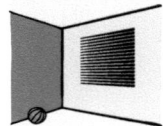

Wand

wall

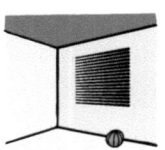

Decke

ceiling

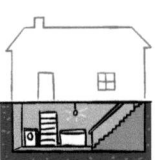

Keller

cellar

Sauna

sauna

Balkon

balcony

Terrasse

terrace

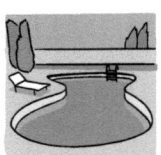

Schwimmbad

pool

Rasenmäher

lawn mower

Bettbezug

sheet

Bettdecke

bedspread

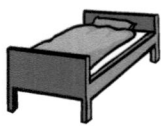

Bett

bed

Besen

broom

Eimer

bucket

Schalter

switch

Wohnzimmer
living room

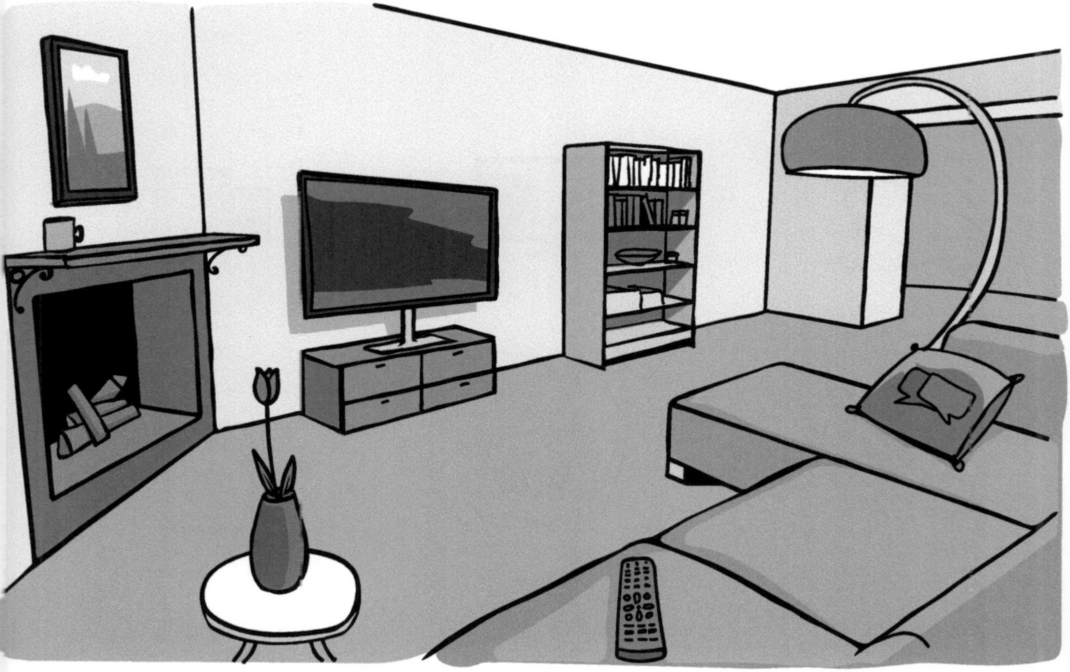

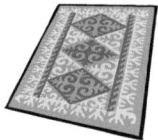

Teppich

carpet

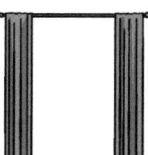

Vorhang

drape

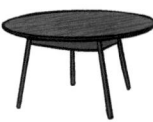

Tisch

table

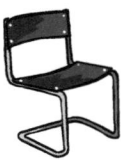

Stuhl

chair

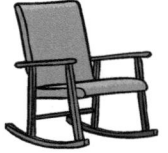

Schaukelstuhl

rocking chair

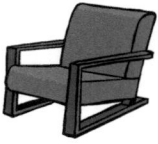

Sessel

armchair

Buch

book

Decke

blanket

Dekoration

decoration

Feuerholz

firewood

Film

film

Stereoanlage

stereo system

Schlüssel

key

Zeitung

newspaper

Gemälde

painting

Poster

poster

Radio

radio

Notizblock

notebook

Staubsauger

vacuum cleaner

Kaktus

cactus

Kerze

candle

Küche
kitchen

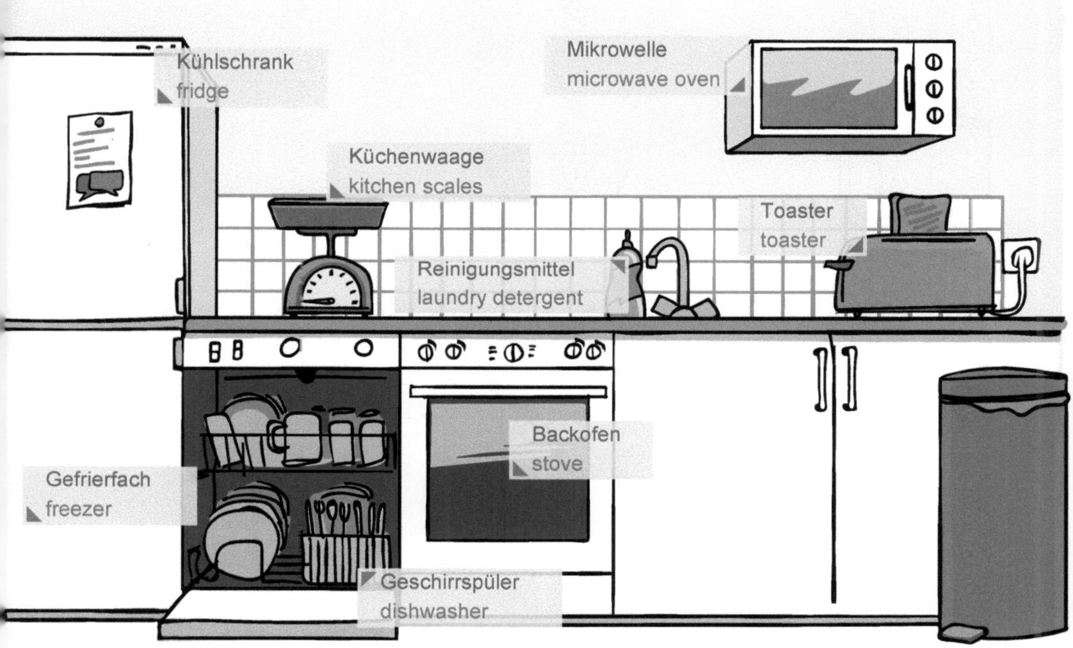
Kühlschrank
fridge
Mikrowelle
microwave oven
Küchenwaage
kitchen scales
Toaster
toaster
Reinigungsmittel
laundry detergent
Backofen
stove
Gefrierfach
freezer
Geschirrspüler
dishwasher

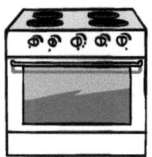

Herd

cooker

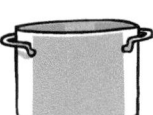

Topf

pot

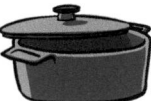

Eisentopf

cast-iron pot

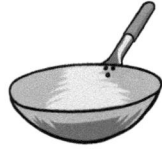

Wok / Kadai

wok / kadai

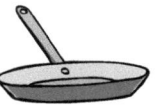

Pfanne

pan

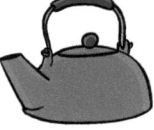

Wasserkocher

kettle

Dampfgarer

steamer

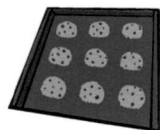

Backblech

baking tray

Geschirr

crockery

Becher

mug

Schale

bowl

Essstäbchen

chopsticks

Suppenkelle

ladle

Pfannenwender

spatula

Schneebesen

whisk

Kochsieb

strainer

Sieb

sieve

Reibe

grater

Mörser

mortar

Grill

barbecue

Feuerstelle

fireplace

Schneidebrett

chopping board

Nudelholz

rolling pin

Korkenzieher

corkscrew

Dose

can

Dosenöffner

can opener

Topflappen

oven cloth

Waschbecken

sink

Bürste

brush

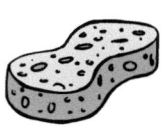

Schwamm

sponge

Mixer

blender

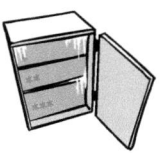

Gefriertruhe

deep freezer

Babyflasche

baby bottle

Wasserhahn

tap

Badezimmer
bathroom

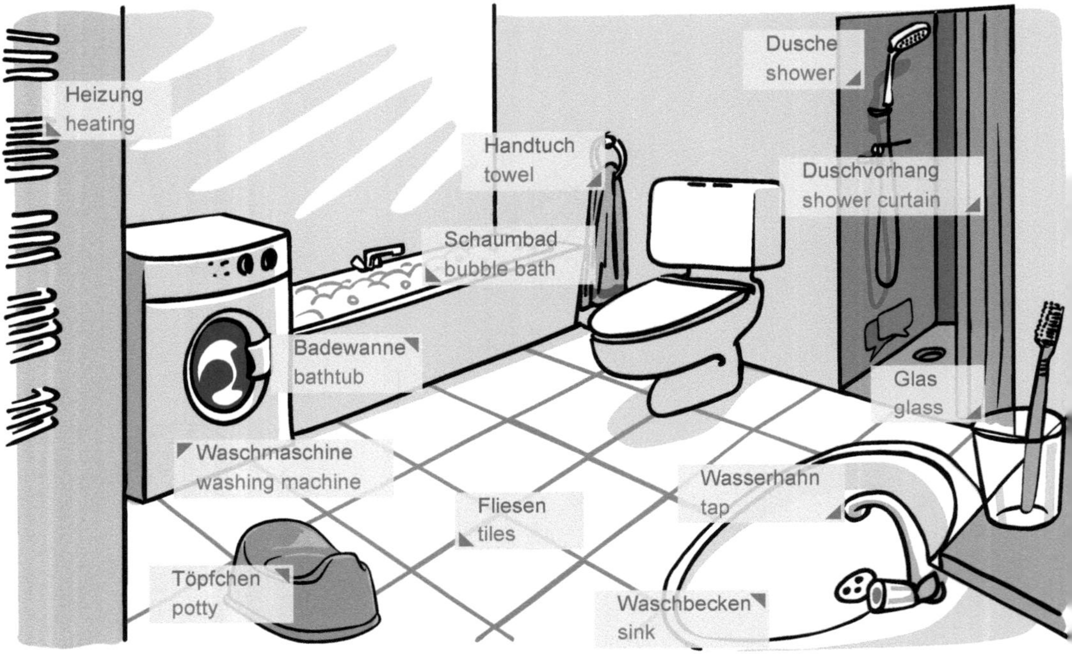

Heizung
heating

Dusche
shower

Handtuch
towel

Duschvorhang
shower curtain

Schaumbad
bubble bath

Badewanne
bathtub

Glas
glass

Waschmaschine
washing machine

Fliesen
tiles

Wasserhahn
tap

Töpfchen
potty

Waschbecken
sink

Toilette	Hocktoilette	Bidet
toilet	squat toilet	bidet
Pissoir	Toilettenpapier	Toilettenbürste
urinal	toilet paper	toilet brush

Zahnbürste

toothbrush

Zahnpasta

toothpaste

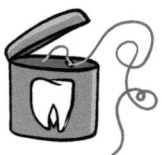

Zahnseide

dental floss

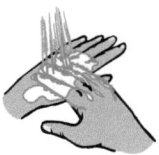

waschen

wash

Handbrause

hand shower

Intimdusche

douche

Waschschüssel

basin

Rückenbürste

back brush

Seife

soap

Duschgel

shower gel

Shampoo

shampoo

Waschlappen

flannel

Abfluss

drain

Creme

creme

Deodorant

deodorant

Spiegel

mirror

Kosmetikspiegel

hand mirror

Rasierer

razor

Rasierschaum

shaving foam

Rasierwasser

aftershave

Kamm

comb

Bürste

brush

Föhn

hair-dryer

Haarspray

hairspray

Makeup

makeup

Lippenstift

lipstick

Nagellack

nail varnish

Watte

cotton wool

Nagelschere

nail scissors

Parfum

perfume

Kulturbeutel

washbag

Hocker

stool

Waage

weighing scales

Bademantel

bathrobe

Gummihandschuhe

rubber gloves

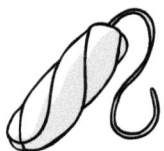

Tampon

tampon

Damenbinde

sanitary towel

Chemietoilette

chemical toilet

Kinderzimmer
kids room

Wecker
alarm clock
Kuscheltier
cuddly toy
Spielzeugauto
toy car
Rassel
rattle
Puppenhaus
doll's house
Geschenk
present

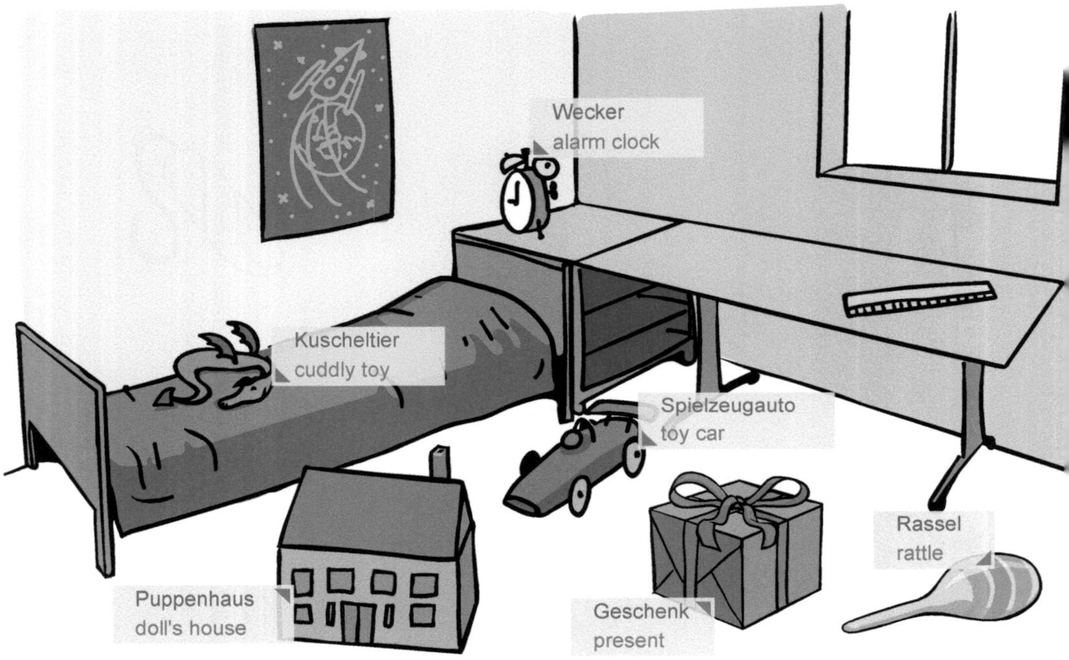

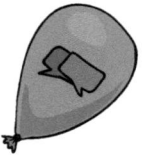

Ballon

balloon

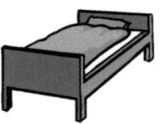

Bett

bed

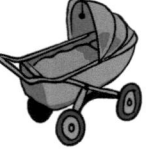

Kinderwagen

stroller

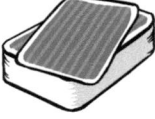

Kartenspiel

deck of cards

Puzzle

jigsaw

SUPER
MEGA

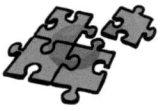

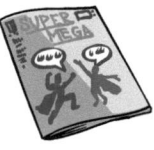

Comic

comic

Legosteine

lego bricks

Bausteine

toy blocks

Action Figur

action figure

Strampelanzug

romper suit

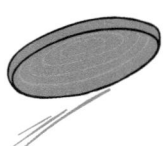

Frisbee

frisbee

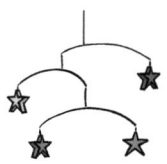

Mobile

mobile

Brettspiel

board game

Würfel

dice

Modelleisenbahn

model train set

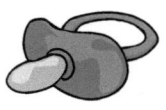

Schnuller

pacifier

Party

party

Bilderbuch

picture book

Ball

ball

Puppe

doll

spielen

play

Sandkasten

sandpit

Schaukel

swing

Spielzeug

toys

Spielkonsole

video game console

Dreirad

tricycle

Teddy

teddy bear

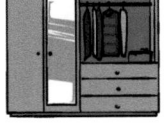

Kleiderschrank

wardrobe

Kleidung
clothing

Socken

socks

Strümpfe

stockings

Strumpfhose

tights

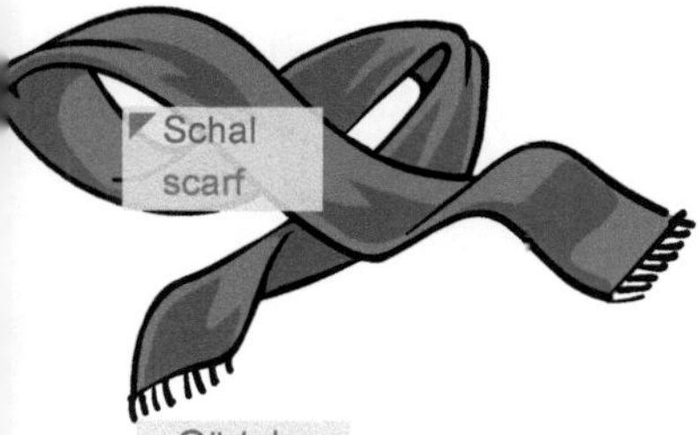

Schal
scarf

Gürtel
belt

Regenschirm
umbrella

T-Shirt
t-shirt

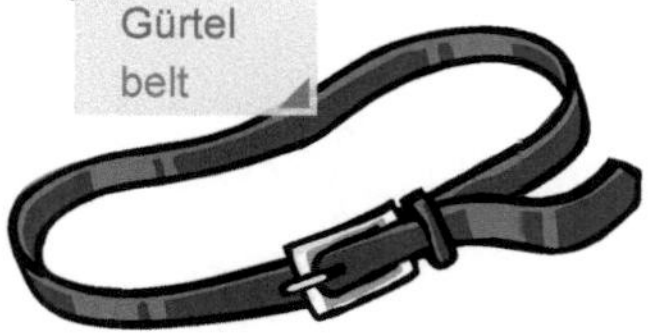

Turnschuhe
sneakers

Stiefel
boots

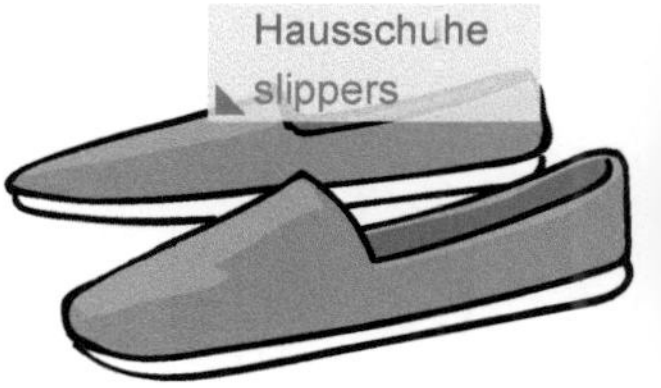

Hausschuhe
slippers

Sandalen
········
sandals

Schuhe
········
shoes

Gummistiefel
········
rubber boots

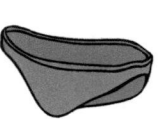

Unterhose
········
underwear

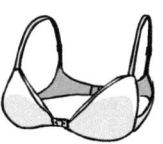

Büstenhalter
········
bra

Unterhemd
········
undershirt

Body
body

Hose
pants

Jeans
jeans

Rock
skirt

Bluse
blouse

Hemd
shirt

Pullover
pullover

Kapuzenpullover
sweater

Blazer
blazer

Jacke
jacket

Mantel
coat

Regenmantel
raincoat

Kostüm
costume

Kleid
dress

Hochzeitskleid
wedding dress

Kleidung - clothing

Anzug

suit

Nachthemd

nightgown

Schlafanzug

pajamas

Sari

sari

Kopftuch

headscarf

Turban

turban

Burka

burka

Kaftan

kaftan

Abaya

abaya

Badeanzug

swimsuit

Badehose

trunks

Kurze Hose

shorts

Trainingsanzug

tracksuit

Schürze

apron

Handschuhe

gloves

Knopf

button

Brille

glasses

Armband

bracelet

Halskette

necklace

Ring

ring

Ohrring

earring

Mütze

cap

Kleiderbügel

coat hanger

Hut

hat

Krawatte

tie

Reißverschluss

zip

Helm

helmet

Hosenträger

braces

Schuluniform

school uniform

Uniform

uniform

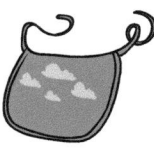

Lätzchen

bib

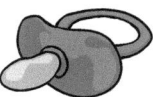

Schnuller

pacifier

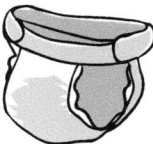

Windel

diaper

Büro
office

Server
server
Aktenschrank
filing cabinet
Drucker
printer
Papier
paper
Monitor
monitor
Maus
mouse
Schreibtisch
desk
Ordner
folder
Tastatur
keyboard
Papierkorb
waste-paper basket
Computer
computer
Stuhl
chair

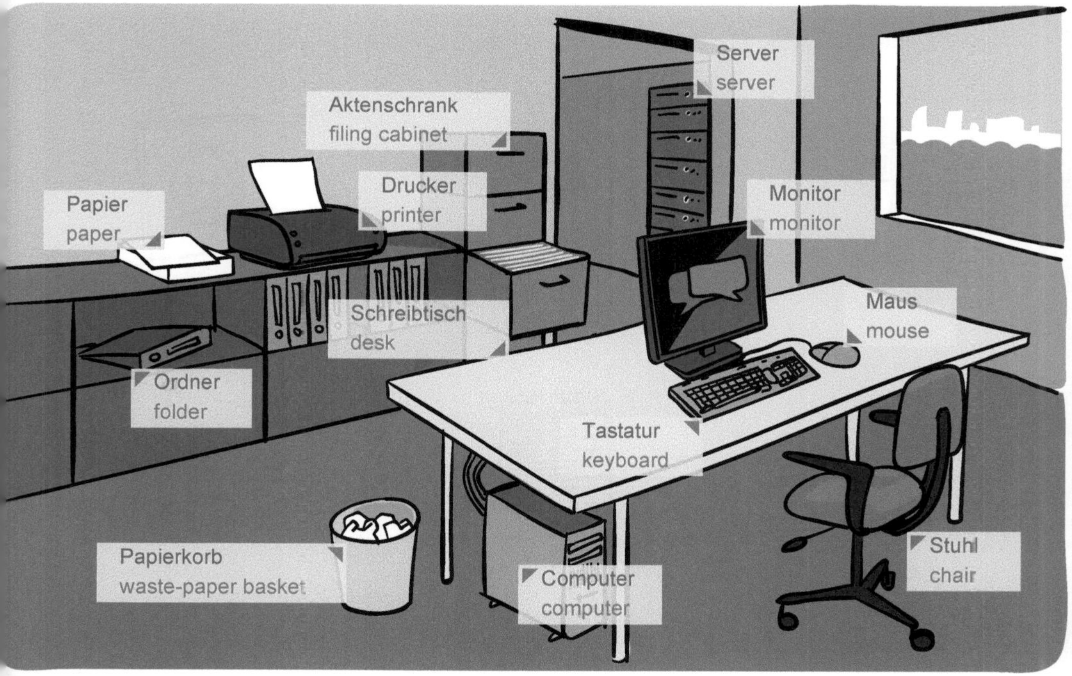

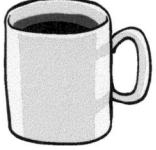

Kaffeebecher

coffee mug

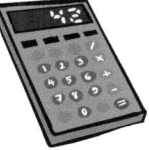

Taschenrechner

calculator

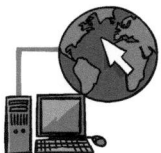

Internet

internet

Laptop

laptop

Brief

letter

Nachricht

message

Handy

cell phone

Netzwerk

network

Kopierer

photocopier

Software

software

Telefon

telephone

Steckdose

plug socket

Fax

fax machine

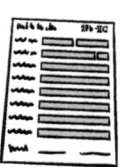

Formular

form

Dokument

document

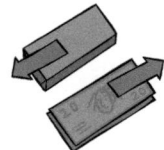

kaufen

buy

bezahlen

pay

handeln

trade

Geld

money

Dollar

dollar

Euro

euro

Yen

yen

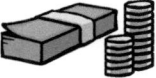

Rubel

rouble

Franken

Swiss franc

Renminbi Yuan

renminbi yuan

Rupie

rupee

Geldautomat

cash point

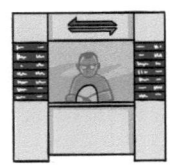

Wechselstube

currency exchange office

Gold

gold

Silber

silver

Öl

oil

Energie

energy

Preis

price

Vertrag

contract

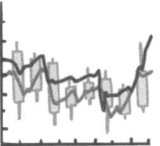

Steuer

tax

Aktie

stock

arbeiten

work

Angestellter

employee

Arbeitgeber

employer

Fabrik

factory

Geschäft

shop

Polizist
police officer

Feuerwehrmann
fireman

Koch
cook

Arzt
doctor

Pilot
pilot

Gärtner

gardener

Tischler

carpenter

Näherin

seamstress

Richter

judge

Chemiker

chemist

Schauspieler

actor

Busfahrer

bus driver

Taxifahrer

taxi driver

Fischer

fisherman

Putzfrau

cleaning lady

Dachdecker

roofer

Kellner

waiter

Jäger

hunter

Maler

painter

Bäcker

baker

Elektriker

electrician

Bauarbeiter

builder

Ingenieur

engineer

Schlachter

butcher

Klempner

plumber

Postbote

postman

Soldat

soldier

Architekt

architect

Kassierer

cashier

Florist

florist

Friseur

hairdresser

Schaffner

conductor

Mechaniker

mechanic

Kapitän

captain

Zahnarzt

dentist

Wissenschaftler

scientist

Rabbi

rabbi

Imam

imam

Mönch

monk

Geistlicher

pastor

Werkzeuge

tools

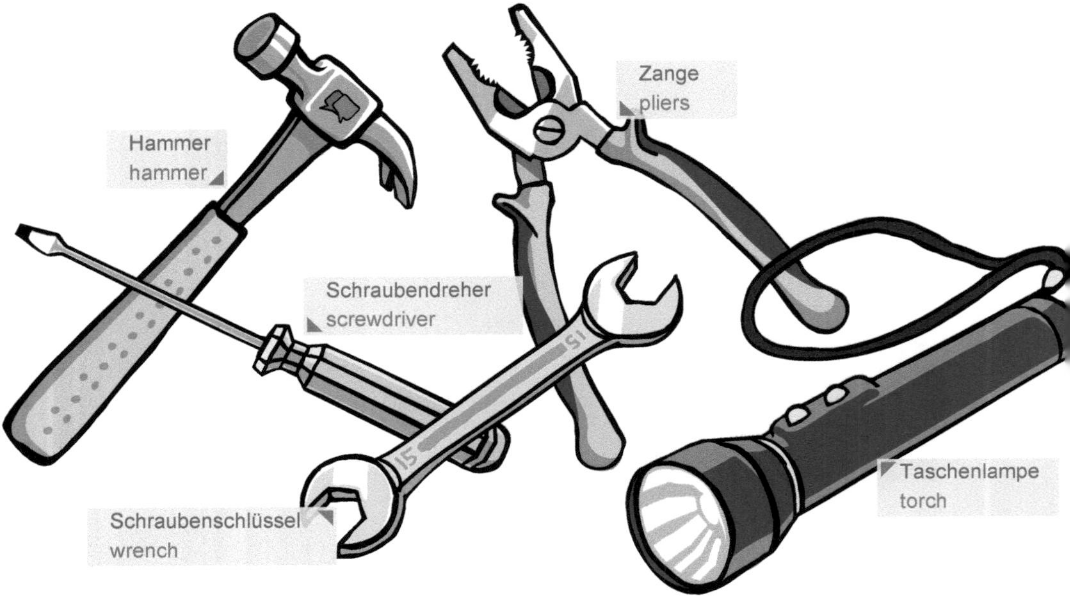

Hammer
hammer

Zange
pliers

Schraubendreher
screwdriver

Schraubenschlüssel
wrench

Taschenlampe
torch

Bagger

excavator

Werkzeugkasten

toolbox

Leiter

ladder

Säge

saw

Nägel

nails

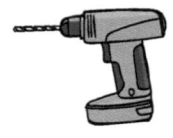

Bohrer

drill

reparieren

repair

Schaufel

shovel

Mist!

Damn!

Kehrblech

dustpan

Farbtopf

paint can

Schrauben

screws

Musikinstrumente
musical instruments

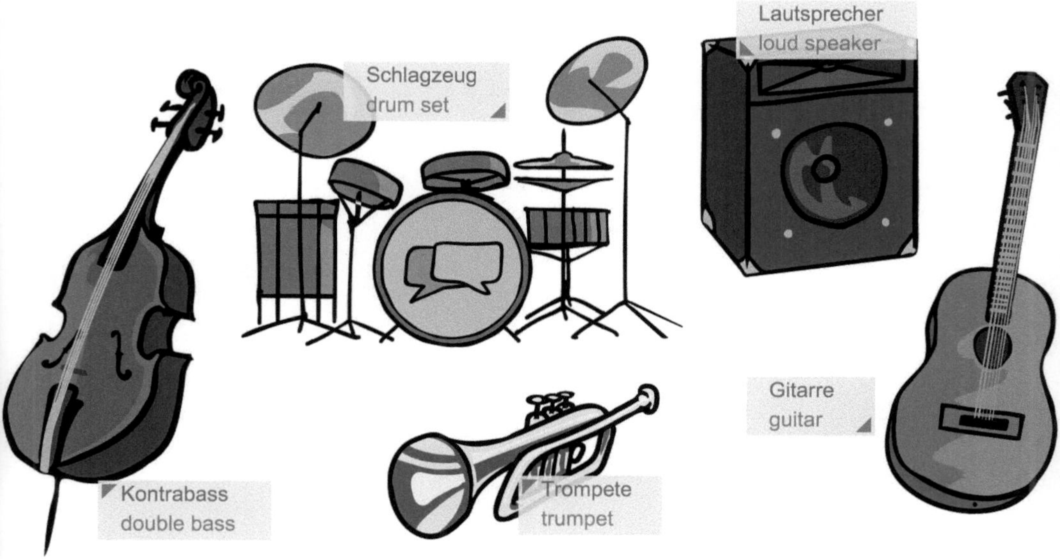

Schlagzeug
drum set

Lautsprecher
loud speaker

Gitarre
guitar

Kontrabass
double bass

Trompete
trumpet

Klavier

piano

Violine

violin

Bass

bass

Pauke

timpani

Trommeln

drums

Keyboard

keyboard

Saxophon

saxophone

Flöte

flute

Mikrofon

microphone

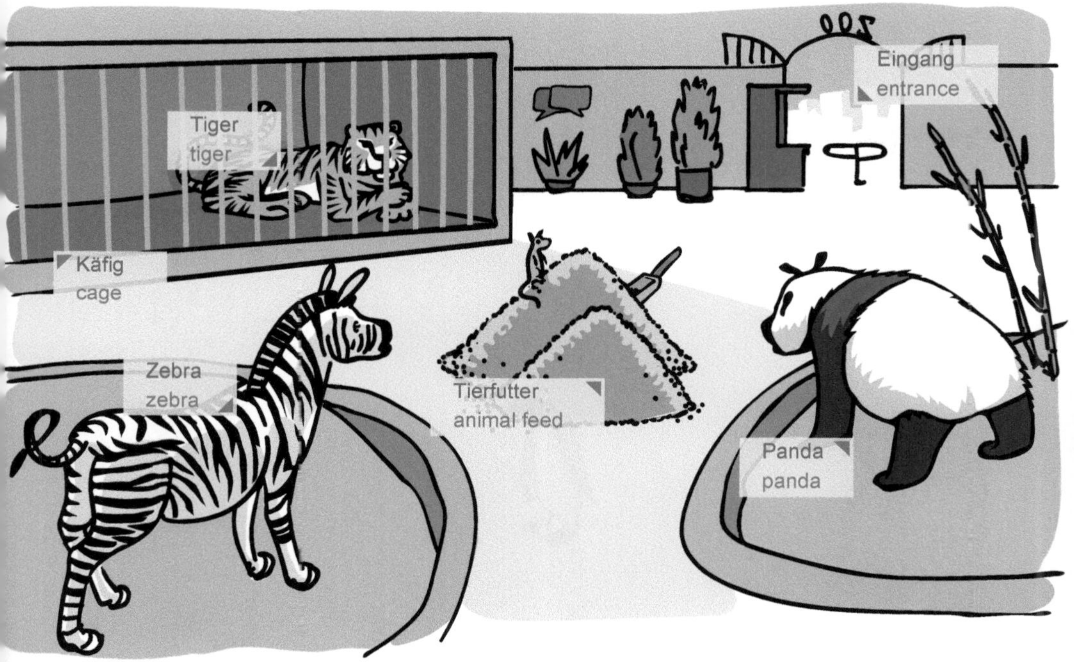

Eingang
entrance

Tiger
tiger

Käfig
cage

Zebra
zebra

Tierfutter
animal feed

Panda
panda

Tiere

animals

Elefant

elephant

Känguru

kangaroo

Nashorn

rhino

Gorilla

gorilla

Bär

bear

Kamel

camel

Strauß

ostrich

Löwe

lion

Affe

monkey

Flamingo

flamingo

Papagei

parrot

Eisbär

polar bear

Pinguin

penguin

Hai

shark

Pfau

peacock

Schlange

snake

Krokodil

crocodile

Zoowärter

zookeeper

Robbe

seal

Jaguar

jaguar

Pony

pony

Leopard

leopard

Nilpferd

hippo

Giraffe

giraffe

Adler

eagle

Wildschwein

boar

Fisch

fish

Schildkröte

turtle

Walross

walrus

Fuchs

fox

Gazelle

gazelle

American Football
American football

Radfahren
cycling

Tennis
tennis

Basketball
basketball

Schwimmen
swimming

Boxen
boxing

Eishockey
ice hockey

Fußball
soccer

Badminton
badminton

Leichtathletik
athletics

Handball
handball

Skilaufen
skiing

Polo
polo

Aktivitäten
activities

springen
jump
umarmen
hug
lachen
laugh
gehen
walk
singen
sing
träumen
dream
beten
pray
küssen
kiss

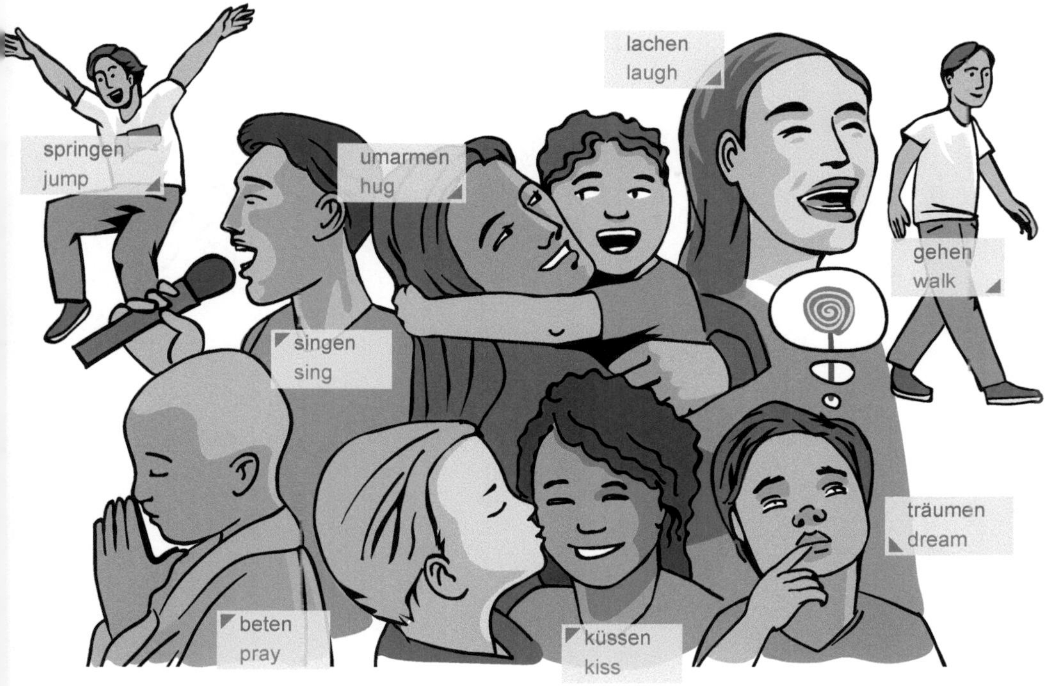

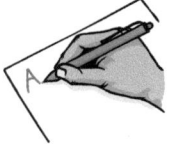

schreiben

write

zeichnen

draw

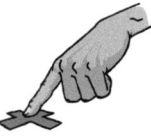

zeigen

show

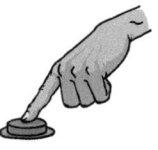

drücken

push

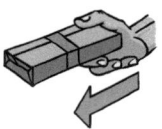

geben

give

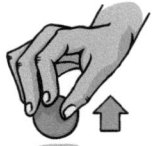

nehmen

take

haben
have

tun
do

sein
be

stehen
stand

laufen
run

ziehen
pull

werfen
throw

fallen
fall

liegen
lie

warten
wait

tragen
carry

sitzen
sit

anziehen
get dressed

schlafen
sleep

aufwachen
wake up

ansehen

look at

weinen

cry

streicheln

stroke

kämmen

comb

reden

talk

verstehen

understand

fragen

ask

hören

listen

trinken

drink

essen

eat

aufräumen

tidy up

lieben

love

kochen

cook

fahren

drive

fliegen

fly

segeln

sail

rechnen

calculate

lesen

read

lernen

learn

arbeiten

work

heiraten

marry

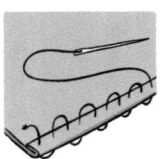

nähen

sew

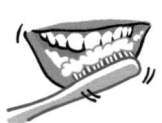

Zähne putzen

brush teeth

töten

kill

rauchen

smoke

senden

send

Großmutter
grandmother

Großvater
grandfather

Vater
father

Mutter
mother

Baby
baby

Tochter
daughter

Sohn
son

Gast
guest

Tante
aunt

Onkel
uncle

Bruder
brother

Schwester
sister

Körper

body

Stirn
forehead
Auge
eye
Gesicht
face
Kinn
chin
Brust
breast
Finger
finger
Hand
hand
Arm
arm
Schulter
shoulder
Bein
leg

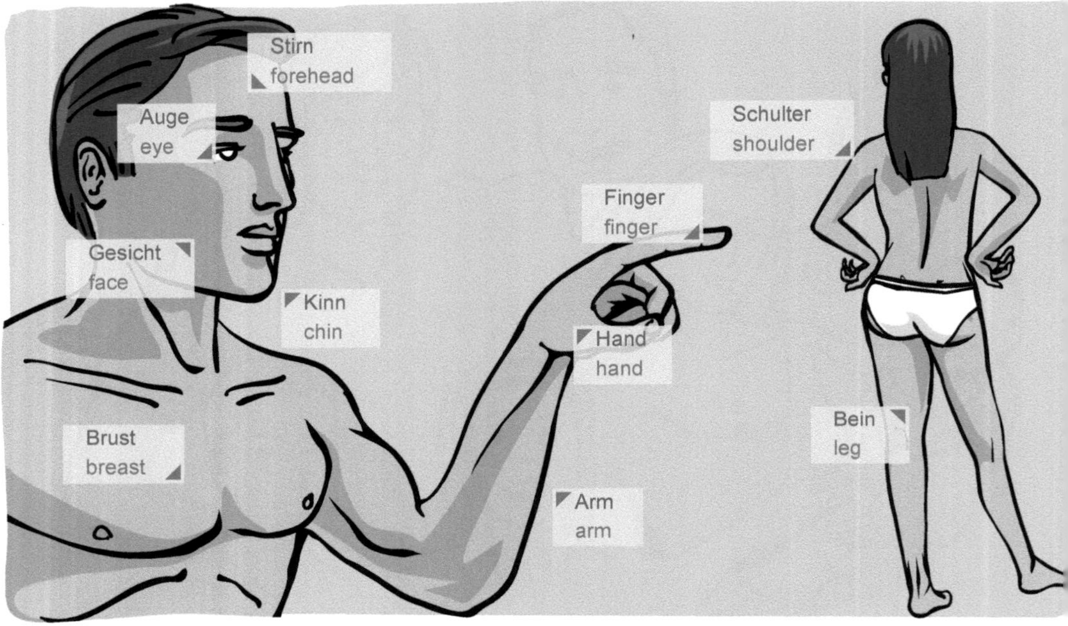

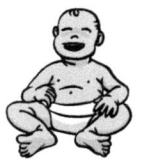

Baby

baby

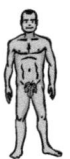

Mann

man

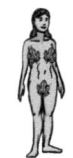

Frau

woman

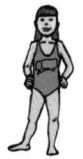

Mädchen

girl

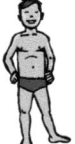

Junge

boy

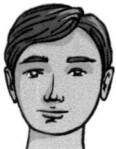

Kopf

head

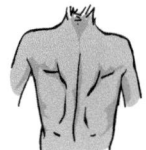

Rücken

back

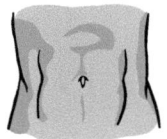

Bauch

belly

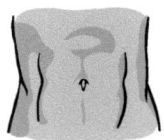

Nabel

navel

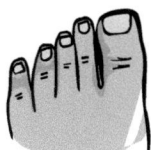

Zeh

toe

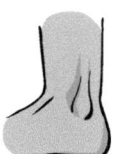

Ferse

heel

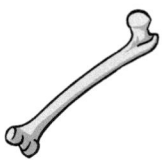

Knochen

bone

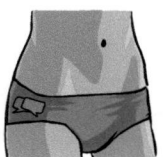

Hüfte

hip

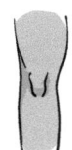

Knie

knee

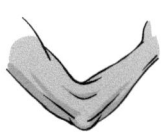

Ellenbogen

elbow

Nase

nose

Gesäß

buttocks

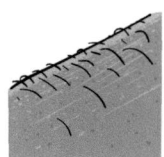

Haut

skin

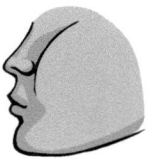

Wange

cheek

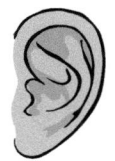

Ohr

ear

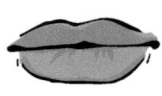

Lippe

lip

Körper - body

Mund

mouth

Zahn

tooth

Zunge

tongue

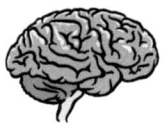

Gehirn

brain

Herz

heart

Muskel

muscle

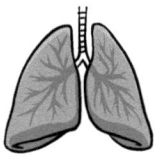

Lunge

lung

Leber

liver

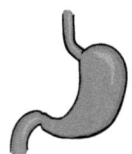

Magen

stomach

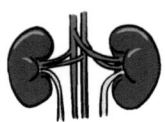

Nieren

kidneys

Geschlechtsverkehr

sex

Kondom

condom

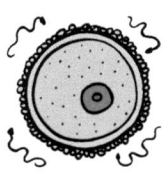

Eizelle

ovum

Sperma

semen

Schwangerschaft

pregnancy

Körper - body

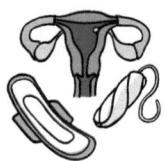

Menstruation

menstruation

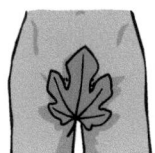

Vagina

vagina

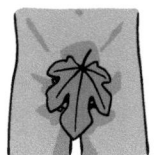

Penis

penis

Augenbraue

eyebrow

Haar

hair

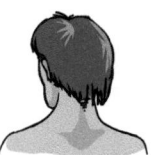

Hals

neck

Krankenhaus
hospital

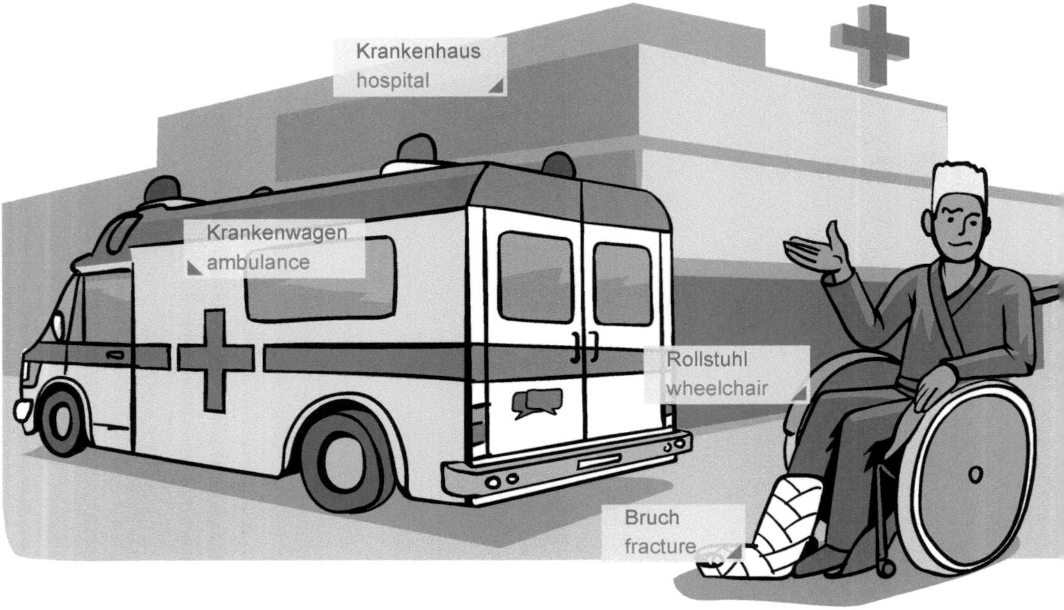

Krankenhaus
hospital
Krankenwagen
ambulance
Rollstuhl
wheelchair
Bruch
fracture

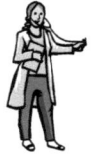

Arzt

doctor

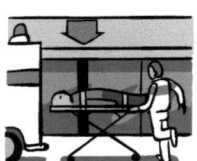

Notaufnahme

emergency room

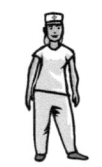

Krankenschwester

nurse

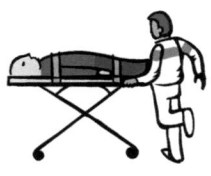

Notfall

emergency

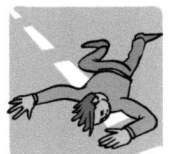

ohnmächtig

unconscious

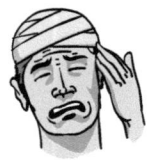

Schmerz

pain

Verletzung

injury

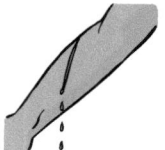

Blutung

bleeding

Herzinfarkt

heart attack

Schlaganfall

stroke

Allergie

allergy

Husten

cough

Fieber

fever

Grippe

flu

Durchfall

diarrhea

Kopfschmerzen

headache

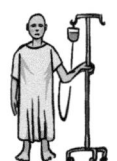

Krebs

cancer

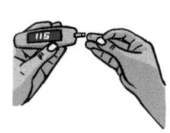

Diabetis

diabetes

Chirurg

surgeon

Skalpell

scalpel

Operation

operation

CT

CT

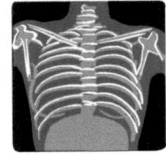

Röntgen

x-ray

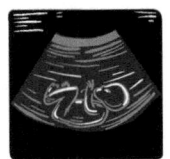

Ultraschall

ultrasound

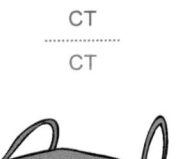

Maske

face mask

Krankheit

disease

Wartezimmer

waiting room

Krücke

crutch

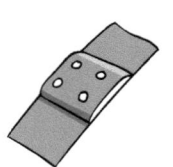

Pflaster

plaster

Verband

bandage

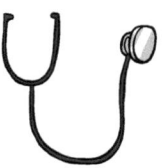

Injektion

injection

Stethoskop

stethoscope

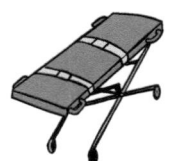

Trage

stretcher

Thermometer

clinical thermometer

Geburt

birth

Übergewicht

overweight

Hörgerät

hearing aid

Desinfektionsmittel

disinfectant

Infektion

infection

Virus

virus

HIV / AIDS

HIV / AIDS

Medizin

medicine

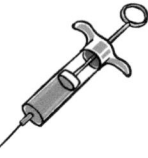

Impfung

vaccination

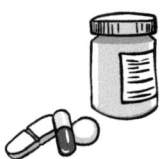

Tabletten

tablets

Pille

pill

Notruf

emergency call

Blutdruck-Messgerät

blood pressure monitor

krank / gesund

ill / healthy

Alarm

alarm

Überfall

assault

Hilfe!

Help!

Gefahr

danger

Notausgang

emergency exit

Angriff

attack

Feuerlöscher

fire extinguisher

Unfall

accident

Feuer!

Fire!

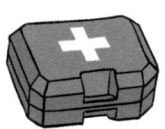

Erste-Hilfe-Koffer

first-aid kit

SOS

SOS

Polizei

police

Europa

Europe

Nordamerika

North America

Südamerika

South America

Afrika

Africa

Asien

Asia

Australien

Australia

Atlantik

Atlantic

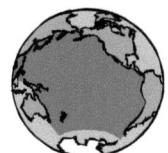

Pazifik

Pacific

Indischer Ozean

Indian Ocean

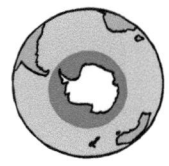

Antarktischer Ozean

Antarctic Ocean

Arktischer Ozean

Arctic Ocean

Nordpol

North pole

Südpol

South pole

Antarktis

Antarctica

Erde

earth

Land

land

Meer

sea

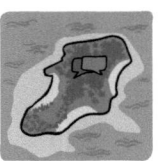

Insel

island

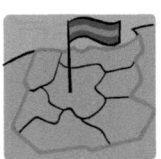

Nation

nation

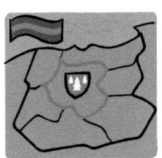

Staat

state

Zifferblatt

clock face

Stundenzeiger

hour hand

Minutenzeiger

minute hand

Sekundenzeiger

second hand

Wie spät ist es?

What time is it?

Tag

day

Zeit

time

jetzt

now

Digitaluhr

digital watch

Minute

minute

Stunde

hour

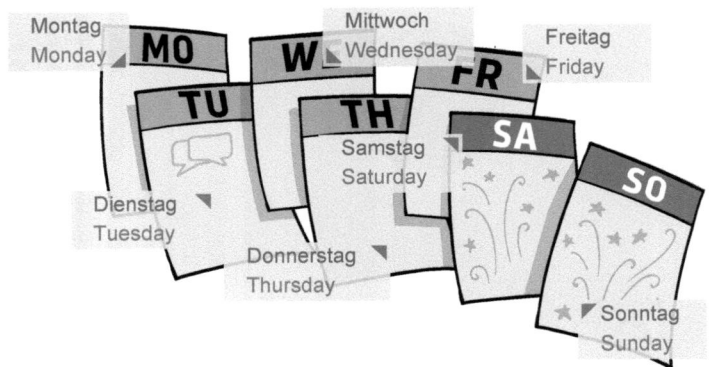

Montag
Monday

Dienstag
Tuesday

Mittwoch
Wednesday

Donnerstag
Thursday

Freitag
Friday

Samstag
Saturday

Sonntag
Sunday

gestern
yesterday

heute
today

morgen
tomorrow

Morgen
morning

Mittag
noon

Abend
evening

Arbeitstage
workdays

Wochenende
weekend

Jahr
year

Regen
rain
Schnee
snow
Wind
wind
Frühling
spring
Herbst
fall
Sommer
summer
Winter
winter

4.APRIL 11°
5.APRIL 4°
6.APRIL 13°
7.APRIL 8°
8.APRIL 10°

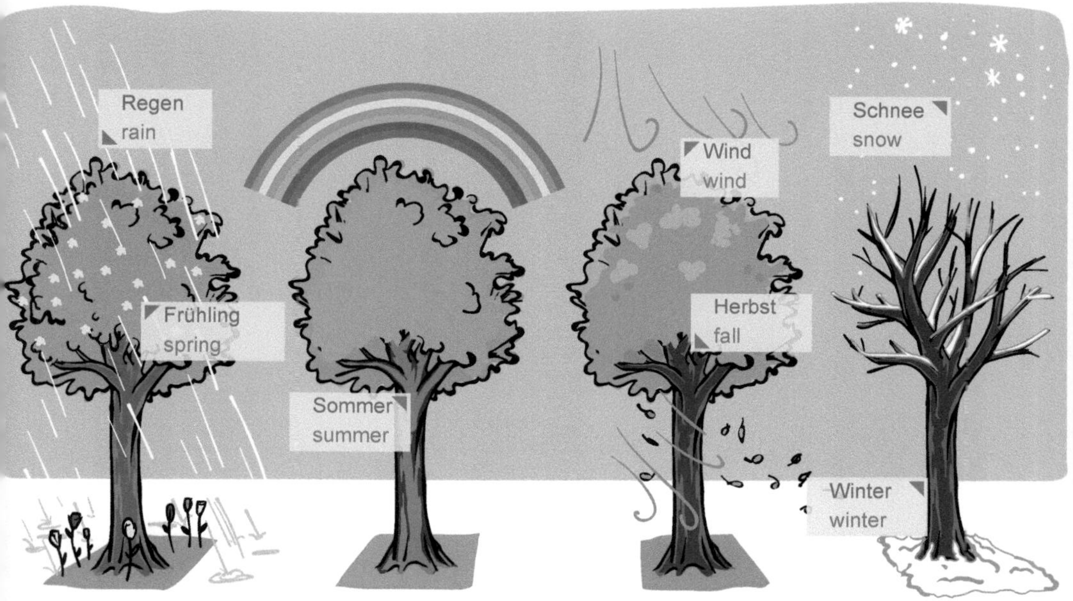

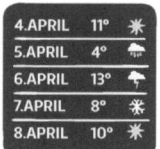

Wettervorhersage

weather forecast

F C
120 40
90 30
60 20
30 10
0 0
-30 -10
-20

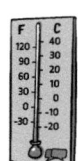

Thermometer

thermometer

Sonnenschein

sunshine

Wolke

cloud

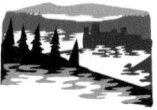

Nebel

fog

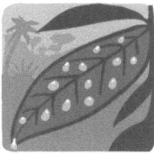

Luftfeuchtigkeit

humidity

Blitz

lightning

Donner

thunder

Sturm

storm

Hagel

hail

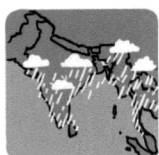

Monsun

monsoon

Flut

flood

Eis

ice

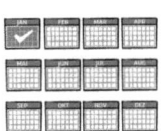

Januar

January

Februar

February

März

March

April

April

Mai

May

Juni

June

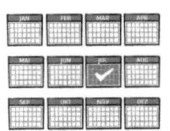

Juli

July

August

August

Jahr - year

September
September

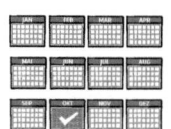

Oktober
October

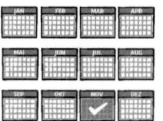

November
November

Dezember
December

Kreis
circle

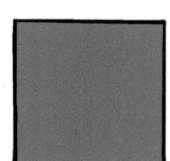

Quadrat
square

Rechteck
rectangle

Dreieck
triangle

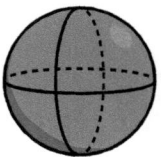

Kugel
sphere

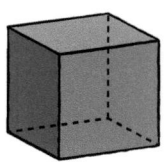

Würfel
cube

Farben

colors

weiß
....
white

gelb
....
yellow

orange
....
orange

pink
....
pink

rot
....
red

lila
....
purple

blau
....
blue

grün
....
green

braun
....
brown

grau
....
gray

schwarz
....
black

viel / wenig

a lot / a little

wütend / friedlich

angry / calm

hübsch / hässlich

beautiful / ugly

Anfang / Ende

beginning / end

groß / klein

big / small

hell / dunkel

bright / dark

Bruder / Schwester

brother / sister

sauber / schmutzig

clean / dirty

vollständig / unvollständig

complete / incomplete

Tag / Nacht

day / night

tot / lebendig

dead / alive

breit / schmal

wide / narrow

genießbar / ungenießbar

edible / inedible

böse / freundlich

evil / kind

aufgeregt / gelangweilt

excited / bored

dick / dünn

fat / thin

zuerst / zuletzt

first / last

Freund / Feind

friend / enemy

voll / leer

full / empty

hart / weich

hard / soft

schwer / leicht

heavy / light

Hunger / Durst

hunger / thirst

krank / gesund

ill / healthy

illegal / legal

illegal / legal

intelligent / dumm

intelligent / stupid

links / rechts

left / right

nah / fern

near / far

neu / gebraucht

new / used

nichts / etwas

nothing / something

alt / jung

old / young

an / aus

on / off

offen / geschlossen

open / closed

leise / laut

quiet / loud

reich / arm

rich / poor

richtig / falsch

right / wrong

rau / glatt

rough / smooth

traurig / glücklich

sad / happy

kurz / lang

short / long

langsam / schnell

slow / fast

nass / trocken

wet / dry

warm / kühl

warm / cool

Krieg / Frieden

war / peace

0

null
zero

1

eins
one

2

zwei
two

3

drei
three

4

vier
four

5

fünf
five

6

sechs
six

7

sieben
seven

8

acht
eight

9

neun
nine

10

zehn
ten

11

elf
eleven

12

zwölf

twelve

13

dreizehn

thirteen

14

vierzehn

fourteen

15

fünfzehn

fifteen

16

sechzehn

sixteen

17

siebzehn

seventeen

18

achtzehn

eighteen

19

neunzehn

nineteen

20

zwanzig

twenty

100

hundert

hundred

1.000

tausend

thousand

1.000.000

million

million

Zahlen - numbers

Sprachen
languages

Englisch

English

Amerikanisches Englisch

American English

Chinesisch Mandarin

Chinese Mandarin

Hindi

Hindi

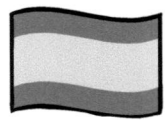

Spanisch

Spanish

Französisch

French

Arabisch

Arabic

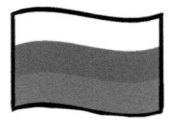

Russisch

Russian

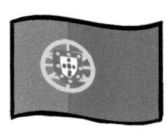

Portugiesisch

Portuguese

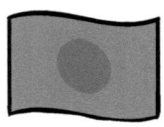

Bengalisch

Bengali

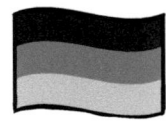

Deutsch

German

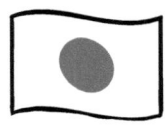

Japanisch

Japanese

ich

I

du

you

er / sie / es

he / she / it

wir

we

ihr

you

sie

they

wer?

who?

was?

what?

wie?

how?

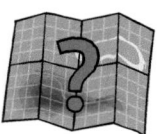

wo?

where?

wann?

when?

Name

name

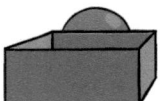

hinter

behind

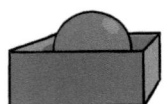

in

in

vor

in front of

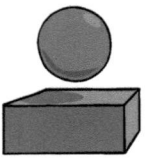

über

over

auf

on

unter

under

neben

beside

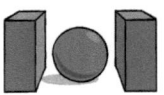

zwischen

between

Ort

place